End of a Vision
The Final Years of Madison College (1946-64)

Albert Dittes

TEACH Services, Inc.
PUBLISHING
www.TEACHServices.com • (800) 367-1844

Copyright © 2022 Albert Dittes
Copyright © 2022 TEACH Services, Inc.
ISBN-13: 978-1-4796-1439-4 (Paperback)
ISBN-13: 978-1-4796-1440-0 (ePub)
Library of Congress Control Number: 2021920073

All Scripture quotations, unless otherwise indicated, are taken from the King James Version®. Public domain.

Cover image: 196-. [People socializing in front of the Science Building at Madison College]. Database on-line. Center for Adventist Research Image Database. http://centerforadventistresearch.org/photos (accessed Oct 6, 2021).

Published by

TEACH Services, Inc.
P U B L I S H I N G
www.TEACHServices.com ● (800) 367-1844

Table of Contents

Preface

A Statement on Sources

This book started out as a series of articles for the *Madison Survey*, a newsletter I now edit for alumni of Madison College and Academy, many of whom still attend an annual reunion on campus and financially support a Heritage House with school memorabilia. They, of course, want to know what caused the closing of the school they love to visit. I grew up in the Highland Adventist community about thirty-five miles north of Madison but went back and forth to Madison because my parents had friends and relatives there. I heard bits and pieces of the Madison story through a first cousin of my grandfather, Dr. Frances Dittes, who taught dietetics at the college from 1910–1958. Many years later, I was invited to join the board of the Madison College Alumni Association due to my serious interest in research and writing about the fascinating people composing the Madison story. I then joined the board of the Layman Foundation, the financial arm of old Madison, and discovered in its archives a rich treasure trove of board minutes and documents detailing what happened during these final years. Most of the information in this book comes from the Layman Foundation files in its Collegedale, Tennessee, headquarters and the 1945–1964 *Madison Surveys* as indicated in the narrative.

These facts and figures should answer questions people may have had on the closing of Madison College.

Madison College campus at the unfolding of this story.

Introduction

In the September 29, 1910, edition of the *Review and Herald*, E. A. Sutherland wrote, "When the land of Canaan was divided among the children of Israel, there was a considerable part of the inheritance of each tribe that remained in the possession of the Canaanites. The Lord left these Canaanites in the land to prove the generation of Israelites that was too young to fight in the days of Joshua. See Judges 3."

He then applied this principle to the work he and his associates had begun in Madison, Tennessee, six years before. "This Canaan experience is an example of the thorough and effective manner of God's teaching. 'Behold, God exalteth by his power: who teacheth like him?' Job 36:22. He might easily have removed all the Canaanites; but he saw that the development of Israel depended upon their making an effort to drive out the Canaanites, and that certain essential traits would be lacking in the character of the younger Israelites if they did not have this experience."

Sutherland identified himself with this generation following Joshua in his part in carrying on the work of Seventh-day Adventist pioneers. "When the third angel's message was first given, the pioneers did the same kind of work as that done by Joshua and his associates in Canaan. The Lord gave these pioneers the essential principles of the third angel's message, but he intended that the younger ones following should continue to develop the work. God did not fully develop the truth through the pioneers, nor did he do all the work required to close up the message. We younger men and women need the experience that will come by doing pioneer work and overcoming difficulties."

And so, he had grasped the banner from the Adventist pioneers and enlarged their work, in his case training self-sacrificing families to work in the rural, underprivileged Southeastern United States and making great financial sacrifices to develop the medical school at Loma Linda, California.

This challenging southern field tested their resolve as much as did clearing the land of the Canaanites developed character in Old Testament Israel or founding the Seventh-day Adventist movement tested the pioneers.

"For years, for example," he continued, "our people have been instructed that two or three families should settle together in some needy place in the South, and there establish and maintain a Christian school and a place for giving simple treatments,—a place where the principles of soil cultivation and health reform could be taught; where the people could be visited at their own firesides, and cottage meetings held with them; and where literature could be distributed, and other work done." His people had done that very thing.

The early students went to Madison College intending to start highland schools in areas with only a token Adventist presence. While Dr. John Harvey Kellogg invested all his energy in Battle Creek, Dr. Sutherland encouraged his students to scatter. The first to do this were the charter students coming to Madison with the pioneers in 1904. Orin Wolcott and Calvin Kinsman, left in June 1905 for Cuba. Braden Mulford and Charles Alden were the next to go just a few miles from Madison near Ridgetop, Tennessee. A year later, Mulford bought a farm at Fountain Head, Tennessee, and founded what became the Highland Adventist Community, the conference school being Highland Academy. Other families eventually impacted every state in the South except Florida, and the Southern Union eventually became the strongest union in the North American Division.

The Madison College founders did not wish to compete with Southern Training School further east of them in Graysville, Tennessee, and so did not actively recruit students from the South. Rather, they traveled to other parts of the country and encouraged families as well as students to come south and start highland schools of their own. Ellen White had been holding up the importance of working in the South for years, but few had responded. E. A. Sutherland wrote in one of his memoirs that some Adventists would go anywhere in the world but the South. During the years of the church expanding worldwide to India, China, Africa, and Australia, it seemed that Adventism was advancing everywhere but in the South.

Going to this underprivileged part of the country required great sacrifice, and that started on the Madison campus. The philosophy was the students must begin by supporting themselves in college, and that meant working their way through school. Sacrifice made the operation of these schools possible. The founders started them on the farm, as directed, and used that as their basis of support. Later on, they added sanitariums, which proved to be a better base of financial stability. A General Conference Commission visited several of these schools ten years later and found their sacrifice "little short of suffering." Yet, they noted these workers did not mind, and their spirits were high.

Though they had accomplished much in their starting phase, Sutherland sensed danger, in looking back on Old Testament Israel. "The younger Israelites, instead of driving out the Canaanites, learned their ways and joined with them. We younger Seventh-day Adventists are in grave danger of having the same experience. The reform was started by the pioneers, but this message is to be developed by us."

Many of Sutherland's students and followers worked hard to enlarge the self-supporting work and contribute to the Seventh-day Adventist church in the institutions they started in many places as well as on the Madison campus itself after he retired in 1946. The challenge facing them required the same kind of creativity, dedication, and self-sacrifice as had been manifested forty years before. They even had some problems Sutherland had never faced.

For one thing, respectability had set in. The 1904 pioneers had taken over a rundown farm with the main house far past its glory days as a fine home in the country. To make it possible for students to work their way through school, they had drawn salaries of $13 a month ($347.71 in 2021 dollars), hoping for more if the farm would prosper. Each year they found the farm income to be just enough to help students earn their wages, so the salary remained the same. The philosophy was if the students wanted to become self-supporting, they needed to put themselves through school.

Now beautiful, well-equipped classrooms and buildings graced the campus along with a food factory and thriving hospital. Such a situation was starting to attract talented people ambitious for their own benefit as well as those wanting to do self-sacrificing, self-supporting work. A thriving hospital, college, and food factory furnished opportunities for personal prosperity, and some people there took full advantage. Then, the student body had changed. The charter students and those following in the early days went to Madison intending to go out and start Madison-model institutions in various places. Many, but of course not all, of the younger generation coming after the war focused on their own careers as well as preparing themselves to work in self-supporting institutions.

But the overarching problem ultimately bringing the school to its knees came down to money. Dr. Sutherland had moved to Tennessee wanting to add a sanitarium to the campus as Ellen White had recommended. They had to start out with the farm and dedicated the Rural Sanitarium in 1908, a good financial move. It met a medical need of the community and subsidized the school, as well as provided student jobs. A food factory called Madison Foods also furnished work for the students as well as brought in money.

But as the twentieth century progressed, the hospital building started aging. Upkeep would have been no problem, except that money needed for that went to the college. As the 1940s turned into the 1950s, the hospital building started falling out of line with state codes. Pressure for a new or renovated building started mounting. It soon became evident that Madison needed to broaden its financial base, that talent, dedication, education, and self-sacrifice would not be enough. An institution must have outside support. E. A. Sutherland had been able to rally major donors behind him. His richest supporter, Lida Funk Scott, chartered the Layman Foundation in 1924 to give legal and financial support to Madison and its extension work as well as the College of Medical Evangelists because of their need for physicians. She died in 1945, E. A. Sutherland retired in 1946, and those that followed faced a challenge perhaps greater than that confronting the founders in 1904. A personal fortune would only be part of what was needed to fund an enterprise like Madison in the mid twentieth century.

The challenge was to find the financial resources needed to operate in an increasingly competitive environment while maintaining the Madison tradition of operating within the Spirit of Prophecy guidelines as revealed to Ellen White. If the presidents following Sutherland had done this, they would have joined him in Adventist history. As things happened, Sutherland became perhaps the only former college president the denomination talks about.

Just how post-Sutherland Madison failed to meet this challenge is the subject of this book. Excellent people with distinguished Adventist careers behind them took charge. Madison College, like all Adventist schools of higher education, had many outstanding teachers and other staff members and graduated many distinguished students.

My contention is that Madison had such a distinguished heritage and made such a big mark that it could have built the larger financial base needed had the presidents organized themselves properly for fundraising.

The board and constituency minutes on file at the Layman Foundation offices in Collegedale, Tennessee, tell the story, and I have drawn heavily on them for the narrative in this book They show the importance of outside support for a school.

Albert Dittes
Portland, TN
August 4, 2021

Chapter 1

Beginning of the End

On April 22, 1959, the board of the Nashville Agricultural and Normal Institute (N.A.N.I.), better known as Madison College, voted to start construction of a new hospital facility and to hire a professional fundraising team. The minutes called for "immediate steps to be taken to put into operation plans for a central unit from which additions may be made from time to time as needed."

The administrative structure consisted of the ruling constituency at the top; then, in descending order, the board of trustees, executive committee, president, and the three grand divisions: academic (overseen by a dean), industries (reporting to a business manager), and sanitarium (run by an administrator).

This system, originally with E. A. Sutherland at the helm, had worked satisfactorily for years but had reached a turning point, as implied in an auditor's report at an October 2nd board meeting.

"The proposed separation of the sanitarium accounts from those of the rest of the institution has been discussed with the administration for the purpose of seeing how to put into effect the board action of several months ago," the report read. "There does not seem to be complete agreement as to just what this action implies, so nothing has been done on the matter."

In other words, how could the college survive without hospital financial support?

The hospital, dedicated in June of 1908 as Madison Rural Sanitarium, had fulfilled a dual role in the life of the Nashville Agricultural and Normal Institute (N.A.N.I.) which had been founded in 1904 and consisted of a farm and sanitarium in addition to a school. The unique purpose of Madison had been to serve as a training base for lay Seventh-day Adventists wanting to extend the mission of the church into the then-underprivileged South. The hospital played an important role in this vision, giving the institutions contact with their communities and also bringing in needed money. Madison Sanitarium and Hospital not only served as the financial base of the self-supporting Adventist movement, but also helped meet the medical needs of the eastern section of Nashville and Davidson County. Its financial strains would affect the entire institution as well as its affiliated self-supporting units looking to it for leadership.

> *The state of Tennessee wanted construction of a newer building in line with state codes. If the hospital lost accreditation, campus life would grind to a halt.*

The Knight & Davidson auditing firm—consisting of two distinguished Madison College alumni, Kenneth Knight and Ralph Davidson—referred to this weakness in the structure that would ultimately undo Madison College. The school had operated on hospital subsidies for years. The extension units of Madison followed this model. A corps of competent, dedicated physicians had been the key to giving N.A.N.I. financial stability, but they were no longer enough. The hospital, having put so much money into the college for so long, found itself unable to keep up its aging physical plant developed in the 1920s, and the day of reckoning was at hand. The state of Tennessee wanted construction of a newer building in line with state codes. If the hospital lost accreditation, campus life would grind to a halt.

The Difficulty of Staying on Mission

The perplexing problem nobody seemed able to solve was how to do this while maintaining the original self-sacrificing purpose of the overall institution. Madison had been founded to, among other goals, train Adventist families to start similar institutions throughout the South. Such training required competent medical and teaching staff, who could educate people willing to work for reduced wages, putting all they had into the institutions. The Madison pioneers had done this, and many of their students did the same in the school, farm, and sanitarium units they started in other places.

After World War II, the medical personnel coming to Madison from Loma Linda wanted to work for normal physicians' wages. Over time, they became an elite group, dampening the missionary spirit. The non-Adventist Madison community physicians had no interest in doing without to train self-denying gospel workers. They became dissatisfied, organizing themselves to build a competing hospital in Madison.

N.A.N.I. desperately needed to broaden its financial base, especially to bring the hospital up to state code. That required outside donations. The school administration had become aware of this in the early 1950s but had made no serious efforts to generate additional revenue from its support base among the college alumni or community. Some local business people now supported another hospital serving the community, meaning that Madison would have to rely on professional fundraisers and government grants to fill the financial gap. The situation was becoming critical; President William Sandborn reported at the October 8 board of trustees meeting that before long it would affect the 311 college and 110 academy students.

Financial problems were closing in. Business Manager Paul Dysinger mentioned that keeping up repairs and making improvements were expensive. Dr. Jean Slate had made a large donation to enlarge the obstetrical department, but these efforts still cost the institution thousands of dollars. Still, the result had been a sizable increase in patronage.

Treasurer James Blair reported paying off a $65,000 bank note and payments being made on four Layman Foundation notes. "Current bills are now only about one month in arrears, which is a considerable improvement over last year, when they were nearly two months in arrears," he said.

Operating gain for the year amounted to $53,899.70 for N.A.N.I. as a whole. The sanitarium and hospital gain had been $118,052.10.

The board voted to borrow money to clear a $14,000 debt in back taxes and $5,150 in accrued penalty and interest.

An architect with the last name of Crabtree unveiled plans for a three-story hospital building, 270 x 66 feet, to be located in front of and parallel to the present administration building, with no cost estimate given. At a board of trustees meeting three months later, Mr. Crabtree presented more preliminary drawings of a two-story new hospital building for thirty beds on each floor with a $450,000 estimated starting cost and total cost of $1.5 million.

The March 23, 1960, constituency meeting reported that a Mr. Witham had been working on a fundraising campaign for about six weeks. He hoped to raise $1 million right away and $3.5 million long-term.

The college enrollment had averaged between 300 and 400 students a year throughout the past 10 years, with a large percentage of them studying in fully accredited medical fields such as nursing, medical technology, x-ray, anesthesiology, and medical records technology.

The sanitarium had performed well during the past decade, showing a net gain of $1.026 million, or $630,560.33 for N.A.N.I. But the education division had lost $424,179.46. Some of the industries had operated successfully, with the laundry earning a $76,872.16 profit, and the store showing a $41,018.39 surplus. Even the poultry area helped the budget with a modest $514.89 gain.

Treasurer James Blair said it cost $150,000 a month to operate the three N.A.N.I. divisions, headed by William Sandborn as president and Paul Dysinger as general manager and hospital administrator.

But other strains were showing. The constituents acknowledged that Sandborn and Dysinger had carried double loads for the past three years: Sandborn as dean of the college as well as president, and Dysinger as hospital administrator and overall general manager. Both soon resigned, with Dysinger agreeing to stay on until a new hospital administrator could take charge and Sandborn continuing to help with hospital development and administrative chores pending the arrival of a replacement.

As it turned out, the institution would reorganize its administrative structure, with Ralph Davidson as president and Robert W. Morris as hospital administrator who, along with a local board, reported to the board of trustees and the constituency. A business manager served under the president, a director of staff services reported to the hospital administrator, and a treasurer worked under both business manager and director of staff services. Accounting, budget director, and purchasing reported to the treasurer.

Carrying a double load as president and dean had left Dr. Sandborn with little or no time for fundraising, and that had been the real need: either for the college to get out from under the hospital subsidy, or the hospital to receive enough outside aid to bring its plant up to state codes so it could continue financially supporting the college. The presidents who had followed Sutherland had neglected this for the past fifteen years.

Fundraising efforts would now center on upgrading the hospital, which faced an accreditation review by the state. The accreditation committee was calling for a modern, up-to-date facility, not just pledged money for such. A campaign had organized an advisory board consisting of leading Madison citizens. Its first order of business would be to "gain back the confidence of the public and the members of the medical profession who have split away and are attempting a fund-raising effort designed to provide another complete hospital for the Madison area. The

Advisory Board recommends that a committee be formed to approach the Memorial Hospital group in an effort to get them to abandon their project and rejoin with us in providing the hospital facilities needed in this area," the minutes read.

Meanwhile, the college faculty for 1960-1961 had no dean. Homer R. Lynd served as registrar and Elizabeth Cowdrick as librarian. (A July 21, 1960, board meeting elected Lynd to serve also as dean.) In addition to a college and academy faculty, the industrial department had agricultural, engineering, industries, and miscellaneous services providing the work-study environment that had been a Madison hallmark.

But now, self-sacrifice had almost become a thing of the past. Subsidizing the college had become too heavy a load for the hospital to carry, especially since a $1.5 million fundraising campaign had become mandatory. At the local board meeting on May 24, 1960, Treasurer Blair reported the institution running thirty to forty-five days behind in paying current institutional bills. "It has been several months since we have been able to avail ourselves of the discounts," he said. However, he continued, "Madison Foods is no longer running in the red, and it is hoped they will be able to break even by the end of the year. The bakery has also made some improvement and the new manager is working out well. The payroll has increased considerably, partly due to increases allowed by the revised scale."

Blair reported two months in arrears in bill-paying at the June 16 local board meeting.

But the hospital, risking a loss of accreditation if it stayed in its old structure, now dominated the agenda. In order to get Hill Burton government funds, it needed a new 250-bed facility, with plans to expand to 450 or 500 beds within four or five years. Getting started would cost $420,260, including an architect's fee of $25,275.60, money now siphoned away from the college.

"In our present situation, snags have been encountered, and time is running out on us," E. L. Marley, president of the Kentucky-Tennessee Conference, and R. W. Morris, hospital administrator, told the board. "The other hospital group, which we had hoped to win over, are definitely to proceed with their campaign Sept. 1 unless something very concrete develops in the meantime. This group is well-organized and supported by community leaders with financial backing, including the E. I. Dupont Co. Another campaign for a hospital building in our community will definitely hamper our activities in the hospital field."

Time was running out. "Mr. Morris called our attention to the fact that we now have less than a year to meet the requirements for hospital accreditation, which calls for major improvements in building and equipment. Without accreditation we will be unable to continue the training of registered nurses and the operation of the schools of medical technology. Also, Blue Cross benefits will be curtailed."

Mr. Witham and Elder Marley presented some criticisms of the hospital they had heard.

> Methods used in collecting patients' accounts irritate our patrons.
> We are classed as a denominationally operated institution.
> We have proceeded with plans and announcements without counseling with our medical staff, advisory committee, and others vitally concerned.
> We have given an impression of divided thinking and instability.
> Some staff members do not measure up to specifications.

The board outlined the following must requisites for building a hospital:

> It must be large enough to ensure accreditation.
> Those with skin in the game must unite on a plan of operation.
> Any plan must meet with staff approval and the support of organized medicine.
> Dissension on campus must end.
> Dissenters must step aside and give believers a chance.
> The board must establish limits on its willingness to borrow.
> Borrowed money must not be more than one-third of the project cost.
> All of us must recognize that we cannot borrow money for the project without staff support.

Institutional bills amounted to $110,000 as of July 1 that year, $20,000 of which was for the sanitarium and hospital. A payroll increase over the previous nine months, inventory, bills receivable, and the usual seasonal slump accounted for it. The situation looked critical enough to ask auditor Ralph M. Davidson to analyze this financial situation.

They had separated the college and hospital accounting by August 1960, a change enabling the hospital to pay its bills and take advantage of the discounts. But removing the college subsidy from the budget still made no provision for payment of bills accumulated before this separation.

Nevertheless, unloading the college from its financing enabled the hospital to go ahead with plans for a 100-bed hospital unit including business offices, kitchen, physiotherapy, x-ray, clinical laboratory, and surgical departments located to the west of West Hall. The plans, including reconditioning the surgical wing, West Hall, North Hall, and the obstetrical wing, would meet the Joint Commission requirements at an estimated cost of $1 million to $1.5 million.

The board voted to proceed with this construction, with one-third of the money coming from governmental Hill Burton funds, one-third of it solicited, and the rest borrowed. Less than a year remained before Joint Commission inspection.

At the October 17, 1960, constituency meeting, R. W. Morris reported doing all he could to meet inspection requirements at this late date and a normal occupancy rate of 83.4 percent. The hospital had been able to take advantage of discounts on bills payable for the past three months.

But what was good for the hospital was bad for the school, now with 351 college students, 114 academy students, 96 elementary school students, and 21 enrolled in the nursery, bringing the total to 582. Treasurer Jim Blair said that while the hospital owed $20,000 in bills payable, the college staggered under a $103,000 debt, ($892,752.20 in 2019 dollars) with no provision to clear it.

"The budget provided for current operating is not sufficient to cover back bills," the minutes read. "Some adjustment will have to be made."

A December 9, 1960, budget committee meeting suggested some means to bring the budget under control:

1) Increase dormitory rates by $3/person.
2) Rent out the farm, with no cash outlay from the institution.
3) Cut the number of vehicles.
4) Increase nurse tuition from $20 to $30/month.
5) Cut cash purchases to $29,000/month by careful and drastic budget control.
6) Add a flat rate change of one cent/meal.
7) Curtail the dairy herd to meet actual campus needs and ask the herdsmen to manage the bottling plant.
8) Study employee housing rental rates.
9) Sell some equipment, such as a bulldozer, cars, old bus, and two tractors.

The college needed $60,000 (or $520,050 in 2019) by February 15.

A December 15 board meeting reported bills payable to the sanitarium as being current, but people owed the college $70,000, down from $104,000 three months ago, and a bank note of $34,000.

Regarding the budget committee recommendations, the board voted not to rent the farm, to charge visitors more than students at the cafeteria, and to give more study to the dairy curtailment.

Discouraging Money Situation

The year 1961 began with the college in financial meltdown. Bills owed from September through December 31 totaled $81,884, ($709,729.57 in 2019) with college division purchases costing $30,000 a month ($260,025 in 2019) and $31,000 due at the bank. "We only have $1,500 in special reserve," the minutes read. "Something must be done."

Winter quarter college enrollment stood at 365 and 106 for academy, with all student quarters occupied. But former college subsidy money was now going to the building of a new hospital.

At the June 15 board of trustees meeting, President Ralph M. Davidson and Administrator R. W. Morris reported progress on the new hospital facility. "An application has been made to Hill-Burton for $1.8 million," they reported. "Prospects are good, but they want to be sure that we are going to follow through with the project. We were informed that funds were available last year and other previous years when we failed to follow through."

They also had some bad news. "The other local hospital group has been approached in regard to uniting our efforts, but there is nothing definite to report on this. Some of Nashville's larger hospitals being in the field for funds has increased our difficulties."

By the end of the year, Davidson reported that the prospect for a bond issue was good but that the need existed for moral backing of the conference in selling bonds to United States church members. The board asked the architects to stay within $1 million for construction and voted to ask for approval to mortgage the entire institution as backing for the bond issue.

Some recorded remarks from board members revealed tension in the ranks.

- "A good number of these board members are just rubber stamps."
- "If the whole institution is mortgaged, it is the beginning of the end as [if] they cannot pay their indebtedness now, how could they pay off a mortgage?"

- "The Layman Foundation might as well charge the hundreds of thousands of dollars that it is carrying on its books as an equity in the institution, as it has neither notes or mortgage for that amount and would not be able to collect."
- "What this place needs is a good strong manager, not just an auditor who is weak on finances and business management and has no experience in this kind of work."

The year 1962 started with the college needing a $60,000-a-year subsidy. Local, Union, and General Conference, alumni, store, or other industries were some possibilities. The campus also needed $915,000 (or $7.9 million in 2019) in capital projects such as dormitory, apartment housing, mechanical and agricultural buildings, a warehouse, and a service station. An overworked staff just couldn't cope with it all.

The March 3 and 4, 1962, board of trustees meeting approved a bond issue of $1.2 million at 6 percent interest, with the bonds to be issued over 18 months. The first issue would be $500,000, the second at $400,000, and the third at $300,000, with an annual repayment of $110,000 for the first six years.

That decision clinched the future of the hospital. "The board was pleased and very interested to learn that after the inspection of the hospital by the Joint Commission, the report was given to the hospital administrator, Robert W. Morris, that the inspector plan [was] to recommend a full free accreditation for the hospital," read the minutes to the next meeting, held on April 18. "He reported that he found things in excellent condition, and that our records and charts were kept in a very fine manner and up to par. He was pleased to learn that we are planning a new hospital building and thankful that we had things as far along as we did."

Five-hundred thousand dollars in governmental Hill-Burton funds were allotted to the hospital later that year, assuring construction of a second wing that would give the hospital 260 beds, a well-equipped physiotherapy section, and a modern kitchen and dining service.

But that good news left the college dangling. Madison Foods, which had opened its original factory on campus in 1918 and had been selling meatless foods ever since, had researched new marketable food products, but in the end had little to show for it. "They are always experimenting with soy milk, but it never brings in any more cash," the September 20, 1962, board minutes read. "They are always in the hole. We should get someone with experience that could operate that industry and make it pay. It is done in Australia and other places."

James Blair reported accounts payable totaling $150,200 and notes payable amounted to $103,000. "Nothing has been paid on trust loans for about a year and nothing on the Layman Foundation loan for seven months," he said. "Our current indebtedness now totals $250,000 to $300,000 [$2.6 million in 2019]. The Madison Foods loan now totals $107,000 [$927,422.50 in 2019]."

And how could the school and industries come up with this much money?

- Downsize to a junior college and have hospital schools only.
- Develop a technical/trade school.
- Become an extension of Southern Missionary College.
- Ask the Southern Union Conference to operate the institution.
- Suspend the academy at the end of the year or earlier if arrangements can be made to do so.
- Form a committee of industrial experts to study the industrial programs and make recommendations to either close those operating at a loss or make adjustments to make them profitable.
- Turn over operation of the preschool and church school to the local church.

The industrial survey committee presented a dismal report at the December 16, 1962, board of trustees meeting. Charles Fleming, Jr., business manager of Southern Missionary College and spokesman for the committee, found that fourteen of the sixteen departments surveyed showed a total loss of $75,000 for the preceding year, with slight possibilities for improvement. Losses in the instructional departments and large notes payable complicated the operating picture.

Madison Foods showed a $25,000 loss for the previous year, exclusive of the soymilk projects, with an operating loss of $11,000 for September and October. A milk project there owed $112,000, with loans needing to be increased to at least $150,000 before full production would go smoothly.

Mr. Fleming suggested that Madison might better invest its energy in fulfilling a denominational need for a technical school. "To succeed, Mr. Fleming believes such a school must have denominational status with the denominational wage scale, sustentation eligibility, and top financial management and recognition. Without this it would be difficult to obtain competent personnel to operate the departments."

At the February 3, 1963, constituency meeting, the Madison Foods manager reported a new accounting system and an excellent soy milk product in full production, as well as the factory there once again showing a profit.

Ralph Davidson resigned as president for health reasons, and James Blair reported the college division showed a net loss of $65,000 (more than $5,000 per month) for the year ending August 31, 1962. "The loss from August 31 to December 31, 1962, is the same, so apparently drastic changes must be made immediately," he said.

The hospital had given a final $32,000 subsidy to the college and the institution had sold thirty acres of land for $32,000; so the actual loss for the year was $115,000 instead of $65,000.

The situation was desperate by now. "The board has recommended to the constituency that the Conference take over the institution to operate it. The Conference recognizes Madison's large contribution to the church and is deeply interested in the welfare of the institution as demonstrated by appropriations, assistance on Bible teachers, salaries, membership on our board and constituencies, loans on wages and in many other ways. But definitely the Conference does not wish to take over the institution and is hoping some other solution might be found for it."

How had things at N.A.N.I.—otherwise known as God's beautiful farm from a book telling the story—deteriorated to such a sad state? How could a divinely inspired enterprise like Madison, with such a splendid heritage, raised up to train lay missionaries to the South, that had made such a major impact on the Seventh-day Adventist movement, be brought to the brink of bankruptcy? Could God let something like this happen to Madison?

A look back into campus life after the close of World War II and during the years following gives clues as to what happened

Chapter 2

Portents of the Closing

In a report presented to the constituency and supporters of the Nashville Agricultural and Normal Institute (N.A.N.I.) on December 9, 1946, Dean Howard Welch stated that though the institution had a unique purpose, several problems needed addressing.

He summed up Madison's mission as being "to specifically train men and women for those activities in the denomination which will make them missionaries, yet without dependence upon denominational funds."

To accomplish this goal, Dean Welch felt the need for closer cooperation between Madison and SDA leadership. "I have greatly appreciated the experience I have had at Madison, and through the years there has developed in my own mind a tremendous interest in the self-supporting work and a definite conviction that Madison is to play an outstanding role in the finishing of God's work in the earth."

At that point, the Madison College property consisted of 900 acres of land, with an approximate value of $1 million ($11.5 million in 2019), according to a 1947 survey of N.A.N.I. The classrooms could handle a total of 1,209 students in all levels; the college had a capacity for 600 of those in its work-study program.

College enrollment then stood at 229, up from a low point of 44 students in 1944, during World War II. Enrollees came from all across North America and fifteen foreign countries. Academy enrollment stood at fifty-six, and the elementary school had sixty-three students.

This profile summed up the Madison institution that E.A. Sutherland turned over to those following him. They inherited a challenge fully as great as the one he had encountered upon founding the institution forty-two years earlier.

Some Challenges

Dean Welch realized this, noting that "for the last few years, the campus has seethed with a spirit of unrest and dissatisfaction."

One problem was that the new generation of doctors did not want to make the traditional Madison sacrifices. "These physicians had had part of their way paid to Loma Linda by the Layman Foundation, and had returned to Madison to practice," Welch wrote. "Previous to that time, it had been generally understood that all Madison workers shared alike in the sacrifices that were necessary. With the return of these doctors and their insistence upon working on a different basis, came a gradual change in the financial setup of the institution."

"Little by little various workers began to feel that if the doctors could have extra income, that others should have the same privilege," he continued. "The spirit of sacrifice characterizing the early work began to dwindle. Gradually there grew up a system on the campus whereby a wage or subsistence pay was given on a regular basis but wherever workers seemed to indicate need, and if it was especially desired to hold them, extra jobs with extra pay were worked out for them."

As examples, he cited surplus pay to William Sandborn doing concrete work on a contract basis, Walter Wilson delivering coal, William Rocke handling insurance for individuals and the institution, and Walter Hilgers sharing a percentage of collections and posting— as well as getting paid by Dr. Joe Sutherland (son of E.A. Sutherland) for doing his income tax. Additional work and pay also went to some dissatisfied nurses.

"We recite these illustrations not in any way to condemn those who took part in them," Welch wrote. "Most of them were legitimately voted and we do not consider that there was any dishonesty involved in most cases. However, the situation did lead to suspicion. Special extra jobs were often referred to as rackets."

And that was not all.

"There has been a strong feeling throughout the constituency that neither Dr. Joe Sutherland nor Mr. Walter Hilgers have been able to give to the medical division the strong spiritual leadership necessary to make it all that it ought to be as a medical missionary enterprise," Dean Welch continued. "Many seemed to feel that the management of the sanitarium was inclined to neglect or ignore the spiritual and religious program of the institution and expected the chaplain alone to carry this burden. From time to time serious questions have been raised over the handling of Sabbath work. Nurses and housekeepers have continually complained that the management was not careful in regard to Sabbath dismissals and admissions and that inside staff members were the worst offenders. Complaint became serious over the matter of handling tobacco, alcohol, tea, coffee, etc. Student nurses have felt that the medical staff was critical toward their efforts to pray with patients and to do medical missionary work. There seems to have been a lack of confidence in the promises made by leaders in the medical division."

A 1947 divorce scandal had forced the resignation of Dr. Joe Sutherland as head physician of the hospital. Dr. Julian Gant replaced him. Negative stories coming out of it had caused a decline in nursing student enrollment.

In addition, the N.A.N.I. business management needed overhauling. Some rumored that funds from the Druillard Trust Fund, a bequest from the estate of pioneer Nellie R. Druillard, had—in the form of a loan—been diverted from benefiting the institution to helping build a clinic for Dr. Joe Sutherland. College divisions could not easily identify their budgeted funds. "The accounting system seems to be inadequate for our needs as a college," he wrote.

Welch concluded that the Madison enterprise needed four basic reforms:

1. New leadership to give proper spiritual tone to the medical division. "This by all means must involve the position of medical director and may go further than that," he noted.
2. Improvement of accounting and business management.
3. Development of outstanding teaching of technical and industrial subjects to achieve the fundamental objective of training self-supporting lay missionaries to live in rural communities.
4. Control of the subsidiary financial assets—such as the Druillard Trust Fund and the Layman Foundation—in a larger, representative group.

A New Era Begins

On April 21, 1946, a retiring Dr. E.A. Sutherland introduced Dr. Thomas Steen as the new president of Madison College.

Dr. Steen had earned his PhD degree from the University of Chicago, his dissertation being a survey of the SDA educational system. He recommended a centralized organization, including all denominational colleges, with a control board sending each SDA student to the specific school of higher learning best fitted to develop his or her individual talents.

He saw Madison as fitting into the big picture as a vocational school, with eleventh and twelfth grades of academy and freshman and sophomore years of college. His program called for the addition of a number of industrial courses, aimed at students for whom the professional program would be inappropriate but who could profit from good vocational courses.

Dr. Steen planned to discontinue the bachelor of science program after the 1948 graduation. However, this strategy was out of line with the Madison mission statement. In May of 1946, soon after Dr. Steen took over as president of Madison, but before E.A. Sutherland left to serve in the General Conference, a committee on self-work at Madison declared, "The work of Madison is to train people to support themselves in rural areas through agriculture, medical work of various types, mechanical lines, resident colporteurs, health food work, home canning ... to help our people to find employment where they will not have to work under the Labor Unions, and also help our people who need men to work with them to find suitable employees."

The Madison College pioneers, in their careful study of the South in 1904, had noted that the plantation system had favored "educating the classes but not the masses." The children of the planter families studied under private tutors or went away to boarding schools. The others—both white and black—did without. The smaller-scale farmers could not compete with plantations—having the advantage of free-labor slaves—and had therefore been driven into the hills. Their children hence had limited educational opportunities, and the Madison founders trained their students to fill this gap. The result was small institutions in many places.

Dr. Steen's vocational-education plan "gave the original college a severe jolt," according to a history of the school in this period. The N.A.N.I. board voted not to accept it.

This reorganization not only violated the objectives of the institution, but also the standards for Madison as stated by a General Conference Committee appointed to clarify its role in the overall work of the denomination.

Minutes of this group, which met in Kansas City, Missouri, on October 8, 1947, read, "Its [Madison's] objective is to equip and train students as lay workers in self-supporting missionary activities." Needed would be "technical and industrial workers for fields of endeavor best adapted to self-supporting missionary work." Madison "proposes to afford worthy young men and women an opportunity to meet the expense of such college educational training by employment in school activities."

In other words, students started their self-supporting missionary work training by working their way through college.

An unsigned letter to the brethren of the survey committee dated December 9, 1946, cited some problems concerning Dr. Steen. He apparently did not understand the purpose of Madison, which the committee said should be "to educate mainly those who are desirous of becoming self-supporting lay workers so that Madison itself as well as the other units, can carry on and at the same time start many similar enterprises. Its plan is to do this without subsidy from the Seventh-day Adventist Organized Work. This requires strict economy, with a subsistence lower than prevailing wages, a lower sustentation guarantee and a greater call for sacrifice. During the six months association with Dr. Steen as president of Madison College, we have been forced to the conclusion that he is not in harmony with the present plan of operation, which we understand has the endorsement of the General Conference," the letter concluded. It asked for a new president more sympathetic to the Madison mission.

Dr. Steen retired in August 1948. His successor, Professor Walter E. Straw, disagreed with the junior college reorganization. Instead, he granted bachelor's degrees in 1949 and 1950.

The junior college model remained, but it attracted students and teachers unfitted for self-supporting work. "The spirit of self-support has died from the campus," said the report. "The school had an impossible program for self-supporting students."

The Real Need

But Dr. Steen had perceived another incipient crisis at N.A.N.I. In his introductory remarks while taking over the presidency from Dr. Sutherland, he said, "Finances present another problem for us to solve. We must not spend more than our income warrants .... We must offer courses in the college that will quickly prepare people to enter into service, professional, pre professional, agricultural, industrial, and others."

The April 30, 1947, *Madison Survey*, the official public relations voice of the institution, listed a committee on buildings and improvements, with Dr. Steen himself serving as chairman. Other members were Professor E.E. Cossentine, Professor H.C. Klement, Dr. Julian C. Gant, Dr. E.A. Sutherland, Dr. P.A. Webber, and Dean H. J. Welch. Its goal was to enlarge the institution's physical plant.

"For many years Madison has been adding to its hospital and educational buildings," the official statement said. "It can now care for a maximum of 180 patients, and its five educational buildings provide classroom, library, and laboratory facilities sufficient for more than 600 college students. In the earlier years, students were housed largely in cottages. Dormitory buildings are limited in size. Married students should have all the cottages, and many more are needed for employees. Many other facilities are also imperative." The Madison family now consisted of more than 500 people, including 200 full-time employees, 325 students, and some part-time workers.

Making these improvements would cost an estimated $560,000, or $6.4 million in 2019 currency. The board appointed two committees to begin work immediately and make a complete report at the next meeting, to be held July 9.

In the February 15, 1948, Survey, Business Manager Charles O. Franz reported the hiring of H.B. Thomas as hospital administrator and K.C. Knight to head the business office, freeing Walter Hilgers to devote his time to fundraising, to "make known to men of means and influence the possibilities of helping to develop a work dedicated both to the carrying of the good news of salvation and the making known to mankind as a part of the full message, the advantages of the proper care of the body and mind through diet, country living, and wholesome surroundings."

To raise this much money while adhering to the Madison Spirit of Prophecy tradition would require as much—if not more—faith, dedication, self-sacrifice, and creativity as the pioneers had exercised at the 1904 founding.

Hilgers cited the need for more housing, greater agriculture teaching facilities, and more provision for mechanical and technical training.

He went to work to solicit money for the most pressing need—a new sanitarium kitchen costing an estimated $200,000 ($2.3 million in 2019 dollars).

To raise this much money while adhering to the Madison Spirit of Prophecy tradition would require as much—if not more—faith, dedication, self-sacrifice, and creativity as the pioneers had exercised at the 1904 founding.

Chapter 3

The Fundraising Begins

The May 12, 1948, *Madison Survey* announced that the Rural Educational Association (R.E.A.) Board of Directors had elected Walter E. Straw as president of Madison College.

He had enjoyed a distinguished career in Adventist education, having served as dean of Madison College and head of the Bible Department from 1929 to 1933. Subsequent service included Bible teacher at Emmanuel Missionary College in Berrien Springs, Michigan (1933-1937), some time at Southwestern Junior College in Keene, Texas, principal of three academies and headmaster of Claremont Union College in South Africa. Subsequent positions had included being a union mission president and educational secretary of the African Division.

Two issues he faced that year were whether to accredit as a senior or junior college and an acute housing shortage due to a growing enrollment of married students.

A political problem also needed resolving. Two governing boards had grown up on campus. The original founders composed the N.A.N.I. governing board. They had in later years turned school administration over to a mostly employee organization called the Rural Educational Association (R.E.A.) Tension had developed between the two boards because N.A.N.I. held title to the property, and R.E.A. didn't feel it had full authority to govern. It made fundraising difficult because N.A.N.I. could cancel out any agreement the R.E.A. made. Also R.E.A. felt it should give some input to the use of the Druillard Trust Fund consisting of "money from the estate of Nellie H. Druillard to advance the work of the Rural Educational Association and Nashville Agricultural and Normal Institute as outlined in the charters of said two institutions, as may be determined from time to time by the Trustees within their absolute discretion."

Nellie Druillard, well-to-do aunt of E.A. Sutherland, had given $5,000 ($129,574.75 in 2019 dollars) to make the down payment on the Madison property in 1904. Though almost old enough to retire, she joined the newly formed Madison group with the encouragement of Ellen White and used her financial acumen to serve as business manager of N.A.N.I. Once the institution was well established in the early 1920s, she cut back on her responsibilities there, sold some valuable property she had invested in at Teapot Dome in Wyoming, and used this money to start Riverside Sanitarium in Nashville to help black people by training black nurses. When she died in 1937, she left money to advance the Madison institution.

Control of the Druillard money lay in the hands of trustees E.A. Sutherland, M. Bessie DeGraw, and Walter H. Hilgers, with R.E.A. having no legal authority. The trust started out with $79,193.19 at the time of its incorporation and had assets of $167,294 ($1.6 million in 2019) by December 31, 1953.

After much discussion, the two boards merged in 1951, centralizing the school administration.

In the March 29, 1949, Survey, President Straw reported to the constituency that "the institution" had received $23,457.27 in donations, perhaps a good start on the $560,000 goal of rehabilitating the school physical plant.

Other good news was "a substantial gain in operating of $46,086.58, making a total increase of $69,543.85. When we compare that with the gain in the years 1940 of $5,962.76 and 1941 of $5,511.99, only seven and eight years ago, we can see that the institution of late has been making substantial strides financially. Then when we realize that the wages in the institution have been nearly doubled in the last three years, we can see that the increase has been phenomenal. It seems that we have come to the time long hoped for when the institution would be able to on its own earning and keep up its repairs without borrowing money for that purpose. This has been accomplished in spite of the fact that we are obliged to pay out thousands of dollars interest on money borrowed before the present administration took over. In the last 14 years this institution has been obliged to pay around $25,000 interest money to the Druillard Trust, on money that Mrs. Druillard intended to be given to the institution. Besides that, during the same time, it has paid to the Layman Foundation $12,000 in interest, making a total paid out in interest of $40,000 in the last 14 years. What a blessing it would be if we had that money now to begin a new boys' dormitory."

The next year, in the February 1, 1950, Madison Survey, President Straw reported the sanitarium as being "our chief source of financial support." Patronage was at a good level, and the sanitarium had a strong physician staff. All that made possible an industrial education program at Madison College offering training in carpentry, printing, electrical, garage, central heat, painting, plumbing, industrial arts education, mechanical and build-ing trades.

This fulfilled the original Madison purpose of preparing students for self-supporting work by earning their way through school. To do this, the founding teachers had to work for $13 a month ($336.91 in 2019) for many years in order to have enough money to pay the students.

It also vindicated the Ellen White counsel of having a school and san-itarium together on campus.

E.A. Sutherland had wanted to develop a sanitarium on the campus of Emmanuel Missionary College in Michigan, but the board of directors refused. Going self-supporting enabled him to do this at Madison.

In the summer of 1912, Bessie DeGraw wrote about how the sanitar-ium had come about.

When Sister White visited the Ferguson Farm before it was pur-chased for a school, she spent a number of hours on the place in company with Elder W. C. White, Elder J. E. White, Bro. W. O. Palmer, Mrs. Druillard, Professor Magan, and others; and the com-pany ate lunch under the trees in a little clearing on the place, not far from where Mrs. Druillard's cottage now stands. As they sat there, Sister White looked around and said, "This would be a good location for your Sanitarium."

> *As they sat there, Sister White looked around and said, "This would be a good location for your Sanitarium."*

From that time on, she seemed never to lose sight of the fact that the Madison School should have connected with it a sanitarium.

Concerning this, she writes, "Early in the history of the Madison School it was suggested that a sanitarium might be established on a portion of the prop-erty purchased for the school farm." In letters written to those in charge of the medical missionary work in the southern states, and pointing out the advantages that are gained by estab-lishing a training school and a sanitarium in close proximity, in the fall of 1904, she says, "One institution will give influence and strength to the other; and, too, money can be saved by both institutions, because each can share the advantages of the other." Again she wrote, after speaking of the work to be done in the Madison School in training students to be self-supporting:

To this is added the knowledge of how to treat the sick and to care for the injured. This training for medical missionary work is one of the grandest objects for which any school can be established. . . . It is essential that there shall be a sanitarium connected with the Madison school. The educational work at the school and the sanitarium can go forward hand in hand. The instruction given at the school will benefit the patients, and the instruction given to the sanitarium patients will be a blessing to the school.

For the first year or more, it seemed that the energy of the workers was exhausted in the building up of the farm. However, the thought of the sanitarium was never lost.

In the summer of 1905, a Nashville man suffering from some kind of illness came and asked for Battle Creek type of treatments. He had to sleep on the front porch of the old plantation house but recovered and praised the way the Madison folks had taken care of him to his friends. The pioneers started serious planning in 1906 and dedicated the Madison Rural Sanitarium in a small cottage on the location Ellen White had recommended in June 1908.

The little sanitarium grew into a major medical center during the next twenty years. A kitchen was completed in 1922. An annex to the sanitarium was added in 1926, the hospital administration building was built in 1927-28, and white stucco in Spanish-style architecture graced the sanitarium in a 1927-29 face-lifting job. These original buildings were now aging, just like the Ferguson Farm structures had been old in 1904 at the start of the enterprise. The twelve-room structure erected by Percy Magan and his helpers out of native lumber in 1907 was still part of the sanitarium. But lots of money needed to come in from somewhere to enable Madison to stay on mission, and the president said nothing about a $560,000 ($6 million in 2019) fundraising need in his report.

However, the school board and administration still recognized the need for outside income.

"For a number of years it has been very evident that a building and improvement program should be undertaken by Madison College and Madison Sanitarium and Hospital," commented the April, 1950, Survey. "The war years, 1941-1946, when many of the students and personnel of the institutions were called to the service of their country—coupled with the difficulty of obtaining materials—resulted in a considerable depreciation of the buildings and equipment of the institution."

This same article announced a goal of raising $800,000 during the next three to five years, proposing to erect a nurses dormitory ($80,000), diet-therapy building ($50,000), and psychiatry, administration, farm, industrial arts, and physiotherapy buildings. In 2019, that would amount to $8.5 million.

William E. Patterson, a special agent and investigator of the U.S. Department of Justice and Treasury Department for twenty-two years and a student at Fletcher, N.C. during the 1912-13 school year, agreed to take charge of raising this money. By the following June, according to the Survey, Mr. Patterson reported taking in several small donations and a $1,000 gift towards the psychiatry building.

The October 1, 1950, Survey dedicated an entire issue to promoting the $800,000 fundraising campaign for needed building improvements. Students and teachers planned to visit civic clubs, starting with the Nashville Rotary Club. Their program would consist of music and then a seven-minute talk about Madison—its history, work, and objectives.

The issue included a historical sketch of the school:

"In 1904 a small group of educators from Emmanuel Missionary College in Michigan came to Tennessee for the purpose of establishing an educational institution where students and others could secure a good education if they were willing to work for it," the article began.

"The school, originally known as the Nashville Agricultural and Normal Institute (N.A.N.I.) obtained a Tennessee state charter the next year. A rural sanitarium opened in 1908 in a small cottage and had since grown into a 165-bed patient capacity institution with fully accredited nursing laboratory and technician courses. It became known as Madison College and Madison Sanitarium and Hospital around 1924."

"Madison students have always been encouraged to go out and start similar institutions on the self-supporting basis," the article continued. "This extension work began in the very early years of the institution's history and is now represented by many other similar centers located in the southern part of the United States. Many of Madison's students have taken the medical course and returned to the South. Her nurses are in the rural institutions and rural units and other institutions. It also supplies teachers to rural schools, and many of its men and women are serving as missionaries in foreign lands."

Dr. Philander P. Claxton, former U.S. Secretary of Education under Presidents William Howard Taft, Woodrow Wilson, and Warren G.

Harding, and personal friend of E.A. Sutherland, had many good things to say about Madison.

"If you are interested in education or in the welfare of earnest, hard-working young men and women, you will want to know about Madison," he wrote, and described it as "a school that receives no aid from public or invested funds, and asks none; a school that young men and women may enter without money, finish standard courses of study under well-prepared teachers, gain practical experience for life and for making a living, and leave unhampered by debt; a school that has succeeded in making all instruction definite, attractive, inspiring and practical; a school that has succeeded in dignifying manual labor and making it highly profitable both educationally and financially."

"I have seen many schools of all grades in many countries, but none more interesting than this," Dr. Claxton concluded. "Nowhere else have I seen so much accomplished with so little money."

"At present the College with its hospital and sanitarium is operating in greatly crowded quarters," wrote President Straw. "Each year the facility is obliged, with regret, to turn away many worthy students because of limited facilities .... Four of the buildings are for the use of the Madison Sanitarium and Hospital, which is operated by, and in connection with, the College; and three of the buildings are for the improvement of the College facilities. In the past friends of Madison have responded nobly and generously to our needs, for which we are most thankful."

"President Straw had a clear understanding of the objectives and needs of the college and would doubtless have steered the ship successfully along her prescribed course," commented the Golden Anniversary Album commemorating the 50th anniversary of Madison in 1954. "But after two years of arduous effort his health suddenly broke, and he was obliged to lay down his duties. This was a very severe and unexpected loss."

Chapter 4

The Stumbling Begins

The December 1, 1950, *Madison Survey* announced the coming of a new president—Elder Wesley Amundsen. The General Conference session had just elected him an associate secretary of the Home Missionary Department. He had had extensive experience in lay training as a union departmental director and conference president in the United States as well as ten years of departmental work in the Inter-American Division. He would now be in a position to professionally train lay Adventists to do self-sacrificing missionary work.

"If there is anything Elder Amundsen has upon his heart more than any other thing in connection with the closing work of the gospel, it is that of the training of laymen for their place in God's great program of soul-winning," according to the news story introducing him.

"I believe here at the Madison institution are to be found some of the greatest opportunities for the development of self-supporting soul winning laymen, of any place that I have ever seen," he said

But Amundsen was different from the Madison pioneers in that he had never self-supported himself while training lay missionaries how to operate on their own. Being a conference man, he and his programs had always been denominationally funded. The Madison situation seemed to intimidate him.

"I am very much concerned about what is happening to this institution," he said at a December 1, 1951, constituency meeting of the Rural Education Association (R.E.A.), the administrative arm. "There is no question in my mind that we have reached a crisis out of which only God can extricate and deliver us."

The school/farm/sanitarium complex had clearly arrived at a turning point. "Today we are facing our greatest test in our struggle for survival. Just how we, as constituent members and workers, will relate ourselves to the divine leadings of God, will determine the outcome."

Amundsen then looked back into the history, pointing out that forty-seven years before "a small group of men and women came to the

Southland, having been guided by the Spirit of Prophecy, to commence a rural training school for the education of mature young people for the work in home and foreign missions. Later a small rural sanitarium was added to this plan."

He cited an official 1907 report of the treasurer, Nellie Druillard, placing the entire plant value at $13,374.25 (about $346,610.58 in 2019). "Today the total value of land, buildings and equipment is well over $1 million," he reported ($8.87 million in 2019).

He then returned to the present challenges. "I have said that I am concerned regarding the outcome of the present crisis in which we find ourselves, for I am sure that no one will deny that there is a crisis," he continued. "The other day I talked with some of the older workers in this institution, about the work and conditions here, and the following questions and suggestions were proposed. 'You don't suppose that this institution will cease doing the work assigned to it, do you? God is the founder of this work, and He will see to it that it is carried on to the end of time.'"

Amundsen then ceased to be specific but just hoped Madison wouldn't go the way of Jerusalem and Battle Creek, "that institution which was to have been a center of light for giving of the Third Angel's Message to the world is now in the hands of the Gentiles. Its glory has departed."

He felt that the Madison family was "in danger of failing to heed the counsel of the True Witness and thus bring calamity upon us all. It was through selfishness and doubt that departure from the faith came about in all of these instances."

But Amundsen did not further elaborate on what threatened the survival of Madison. Was it leftover tension between the R.E.A. and N.A.N.I. factions? Was the $800,000 fundraising campaign lagging? Did "selfishness and doubt" plague the staff?

He just appealed for heeding the Holy Spirit and said he had done the best he could in the thirteen months he had been president, listening to the counsel of the brethren. He pointed out some positive staff changes. They had a new cabinet shop. Better store management had reduced some financial losses there. The food factory had headed off the danger of closing

> *He just appealed for heeding the Holy Spirit and said he had done the best he could in the thirteen months he had been president, listening to the counsel of the brethren.*

by making some needed adjustments. He hoped that new management would cut farm program losses. An increase in church membership had caused the founding of a second Adventist congregation in the community as the attendance had outgrown assembly hall facilities.

The Real Problem

The committee records reveal the real problem Elder Amundsen hinted at and threatened his lay-training expertise as well as the great Madison lay movement.

A February 7, 1951, report of the Committee on R.E.A. finances to the N.A.N.I. Board, consisting of A.A. Japerson, F. Holland and W.H. Hilgers, showed that as of November 30, 1950, the R.E.A. statement indicated financial embarrassment. "The trend since November 1947 has been definitely toward serious difficulty," according to the minutes.

The following problems showed the need for more outside financial support:

1. No reserve cash on hand to meet $105,000 in current liabilities ($1.04 million in 2019).
2. Only $5,000 operating cash is available, a real problem to an organization with an annual income of approximately $1.5 million.
3. Overdrawn bank accounts.
4. Steadily increasing operating expense.
5. Delinquent interest payment to those who have given annuities and holders of notes.
6. Due dates of notes allowed to pass by without making proper arrangements for renewal.
7. Complaints by merchants for slow and unsatisfactory pay.
8. Upward trend of accounts receivable. $54,000 ($532,878.23 in 2019) has been charged off to bad debts. Some departments carry more accounts receivable than their average monthly income.
9. Steady yearly increase in inventory figures.
10. [The] operating gain of $145,000 for 1947-1950 has been swallowed up by increases in accounts receivable and inventories.

The April 1952 Survey announced that "W.E. Patterson, publicity director of the Madison institution, together with a number of doctors, workers and students are planning to establish a private self-supporting rural institution near Savannah, Tennessee."

The year before, the April 15, 1951, *Madison Survey* had run a picture of the DuPont Company of Old Hickory giving $25,000 towards construction of the hospital psychiatric building with E.F. Swezey, assistant general manager, handing the check to William E. Patterson as President Wesley Amundsen looked on. It had been said that the programs by Mr. Patterson's public relations teams had made a positive impression on the Nashville civic clubs.

The story made no mention of the $800,000 fundraising campaign.

Chapter 5

The Problem Grows

The May 1952 Survey announced that A.A. Jasperson, a former Madison student and president and manager of the Asheville Agricultural School and Mountain Sanitarium at Fletcher, NC, had accepted the position as president and general manager of N.A.N.I.

"The board decided to consider the possibility of selecting as president a man who had had personal experience in a self-supporting institution," the announcement said.

During his thirty years as head of the Fletcher institution, Jasperson had also been active in the extension work of Madison College through serving on important boards and committees. A native of Wisconsin, he had come to Madison as a student in 1910 and distinguished himself at Fletcher.

Jasperson was representative of many former students going out from Madison to start similar institutions to benefit the underprivileged South. Braden Mulford, one of their first students to go out and reproduce Madison, went, along with Charles F. Alden, another charter Madison student, and started the Oak Grove Garden School near Ridgetop, Tennessee, in 1906. The next year, Mulford bought a farm for sale in Fountain Head, Tennessee, and founded what became Highland Academy. In 1908, the Walen and Wallace families left Madison to start Chestnut Hill school and later a sanitarium a few miles near Fountain Head. E.C. Waller, C.A. Graves, and William Steinman founded Mount Pisgah Academy near Asheville, North Carolina. Neil Martin and sons operated El Reposo Sanitarium in Florence, Alabama. The Goodge and Straw families started Little Creek School and Sanitarium near Knoxville, Tennessee. Other Madison-affiliated institutions were Hurlbutt Farm and Scott Sanitarium near Reeves, GA, a school and sanitarium in Pewee Valley, KY, and the Lawrenceburg Sanitarium and Hospital, Lawrenceburg, Tennessee, as well as Pine Hill Sanitarium near Birmingham, AL.

Sidney Brownsberger and Arthur Spalding had no initial affiliation with Madison. After Ellen White visited Madison while on her way to the

1909 General Conference session in Takoma Park, Maryland, she went on to Asheville, North Carolina, and encouraged a wealthy woman to donate money for a self-supporting school there. They found the desirable land and it developed into the successful Fletcher institution.

The work of Madison indeed thrived in many places, but problems started taking over the base. The hospital operation started having trouble staying on mission. In 1946, a group of physician-specialists had formed an organization known as the Madison Associated Physicians (M.A.P.) and leased the sanitarium, for all intents and purposes. The arrangement made it difficult for high-income physicians to train self-sacrificing workers "nor is it adapted to medical institutions of the Madison order, such as the self-supporting units for which Madison trains workers," read one committee report.

> *The work of Madison indeed thrived in many places, but problems started taking over the base.*

Some felt the model fit medical school affiliation. The college administration could not operate the hospital like it did other divisions and departments on campus.

Mismanagement had caused some errors and issues the hospital insurance had to settle, resulting in rates ten times higher than the $500 a year the hospital had been paying when M.A.P. took over. They had to change insurance companies, the situation being so difficult that the hospital had gone without any insurance coverage at all for a few days, a risky situation to be sure.

And then M.A.P. had allowed the hospital physical plant to deteriorate so badly that it would take thousands of dollars to bring it up to standard. "We have been warned that if the State Health Department should inspect the dietary department of the sanitarium, it would close the kitchen," stated one report.

The hospital subsidizing the school caused part of the problem. Madison just needed to broaden its financial base, either raising a large endowment to secure the college or using donations to bring the hospital up to standard so it could continue its school subsidies.

The Survey wrote nothing about the $800,000 need nor a huge debt hanging over the institution.

E.A. Sutherland, eighty-nine years old, now saw a challenge facing the institution as big, if not bigger, than when he had co-founded N.A.N.I., along with dedicated followers like Percy Magan, Nellie Druillard and

Bessie DeGraw, in 1904. One reason they had given up their security in the denominational education system was that they wanted to have a sanitarium as part of N.A.N.I. Sutherland had included a sanitarium in his original campus plan for Emmanuel Missionary College in Michigan, but the board of directors, with Arthur G. Daniells as chairman, had refused to approve it. He had gone out from under Daniells' control and started a sanitarium at Madison, and it had worked out. Ellen White had said that a sanitarium and school on the same campus could be a help to each other and even recommended the exact site of the future medical facility.

But that had led to more sacrifice. In starting a sanitarium, Sutherland found what James and Ellen White had learned forty-one years before in Battle Creek: a viable medical institution needed properly trained physicians. Sutherland and Magan had wound up going to medical school in Nashville to qualify themselves to attract patients. But they would need more physicians, and where would they get them?

Sutherland determined that their only hope lay in helping the struggling young medical school based at Loma Linda, California, attain full accreditation and encouraged his richest donor, Lida Funk Scott, heiress to the Funk & Wagnalls fortune, to financially support Percy Magan, who had gone there as dean in 1916. That meant encouraging her to give $30,000 ($601,338.28 in 2019 dollars) to make possible construction of the White Memorial Hospital, in addition to lots of other monies sent there.

Magan had done all he could to encourage former Madison students at Loma Linda to return to the South after finishing school at Loma Linda, and they had come, some of them to Madison and others to various communities in Middle Tennessee and other southern states. Some were sending lots of patients to Madison Hospital. But their success had brought respectability to Madison, and that meant attracting people ambitious for themselves in addition to students wanting to do self-supporting work to benefit others. Some alumni had become wealthy and prominent, but nobody from Madison asked them for money.

Sutherland couldn't do much to alleviate the deepening financial crisis. His rich benefactors like Lida Scott and Josephine Gotzian, widow of a successful Minneapolis shoe manufacturer, were now gone, as was Percy Magan. The only money he had access to was the Druillard Trust Fund.

"At present, I am anxious to see that the Druillard Trust can help the N.A.N.I. with its financial problems, amounting to $65,000 ($618,000 in 2019) Sutherland wrote to A.A. Jasperson on June 23, 1954. I will pledge you that I will stand by you in bringing Madison to the place where it is carrying out the original objectives which you and I talked over many times."

The October 3, 1954, Survey announced a $50,000 ($476,102.23 in 2019) loan by the Druillard Trust to N.A.N.I.

"In view of the financial stress in which N.A.N.I. now finds itself, the Druillard Trust is willing to grant a similar moratorium for two years on the payment of the principal on the notes it now holds against the institution, on the understanding that all the previous notes are paid in full when due," the meeting minutes said.

The legendary Dr. Sutherland died the next year, ending an extraordinary sixty-four-year career, with his beloved Madison College facing a grim financial situation. His successors needed as much help, if not more than he had fifty years before from self-sacrificing people with deep financial pockets.

Chapter 6

The Noose Tightens

On March 14, 1957, the "new" board of trustees elected William C. Sandborn president of the Madison complex after the resignation of Arthur A. Jasperson.

"President Sandborn has been connected with Madison for half its history, first as a student, then serving as teacher, department head, five years as dean, and now as president," the announcement said. "His service at Madison has been continuous since 1930 with the exception of two years, one when he and his new bride went to Quincy, Illinois, to found a small sanitarium, and one year as principal of Highland Academy."

He assumed his office at a critical time.

The minutes of the constituency meeting the day before Sandborn's election as president acknowledged some serious problems at the hospital. "In view of the need for repairs and new construction of the sanitarium and hospital, definite steps need to be taken to remedy the situation and to proceed with the plans as this seems wise," the minutes read.

The brief constituency meeting report in the April 1957 Survey told of "a wholesome discussion of Madison's problems and of her objectives .... The challenge of some pointed talks was met by humble and whole-hearted determination to follow on fully in the paths of God's Leading."

They said nothing about the $800,000 need to upgrade aging buildings.

One of the first things Dr. Sandborn did after taking office was to promote the latest Madison unit in Savannah, Tennessee, called Harbert Hills Academy. Four self-sacrificing families—Nielsens, Pattersons, Cheevers, and Dickmans—were keeping the Madison tradition alive by going somewhere with no official Adventist presence as lay missionaries. Dr. Sandborn encouraged Survey readers to send money to Harbert Hills to help meet the startup needs such as a cow barn, mower, cultivator, hand tools, schoolroom desks, library books, filing cabinets, and single beds for student rooms.

He didn't ask the readers to donate any money to Madison but did announce a remodeling of West and North Halls and acknowledged "many of the earliest buildings are becoming old and worn out, in some cases out-moded." The sanitarium was now nearly fifty years old, having been dedicated in 1908. The May 19, 1958, Survey did announce a $20,000 ($177,261.59 in 2019) gift for hospital rehabilitation from The Dupont Company.

But the N.A.N.I. Board was still struggling to find a way to come up with the huge sums needed within the context of the "basic philosophy of the Madison institution" as well as determine the extent of expansion and plans, not to mention plans for financing the needed new building.

"[A]n increasing emphasis should be placed on the original assignment given to Madison by divine inspiration; namely, the training of a great army of lay people for active and practical lives of missionary service as teachers, nurses, medical workers and leaders in agricultural and industrial activities, as well as other lines of missionary service," the report reads. "This philosophy is in the Ellen White writings."

"We feel to especially emphasize the necessity of constantly keeping in mind, in both the training program and in later service, the spiritual and soul-winning aspect of the work entrusted to us."

Other needs were to restudy the possibility of instituting a larger lay-worker training program, keep close ties to the denomination, and offer more vocational and industrial training combined with effective soul winning.

Everyone agreed philosophically about the need to adhere to the original Madison mission, something those in charge were finding hard to do. In a Sabbath morning sermon to a January 1958 meeting of the Laymen's Extension League Executive Committee, President Sandborn expressed this difficulty.

"President Sandborn recognized the fact that Madison is not now conforming fully to her prescribed blueprint," wrote the February 1958 *Madison Survey* account of this sermon, calling it "less a sermon than an introspection, a confession, and a pledge."

"The best evidence of this is the fact that too few of her students are committed to her one task—that of training men and women for the great Self-supporting branch of God's work, and inculcating in them the spirit of sacrifice and devotion and selfless service on which that work was established; and too many of her students get their education and then leave her halls to go into lucrative employment that has not the remotest relation to the great work to which Madison was dedicated."

Dr. Sandborn fully recognized this need and "pledged his unyielding loyalty to these principles and assured the group that he and his coworkers in Madison's present leadership would faithfully and persistently promote these traditional objectives until Madison will stand forth as a great beacon light pointing the way to a larger and more effective ministry in the Self-supporting institutional work."

Maintaining allegiance to these high ideals and coming up with enough money to meet the growing need for a first-rate medical institution was a tremendous challenge indeed. On July 23-24, 1958, a special committee on basic philosophy and future plans announced the construction of a $500,000 ($4.43 million in 2019) structure "between the present Administration Building and the Sanitarium Parlor with a surgical suite and some patient rooms on the second floor and a first floor of patient rooms." The board, however, didn't mention self-sacrifice but voted "to ask for a survey by a fundraising company to determine the financial assistance potential of the community and otherwise."

Meanwhile, the college's financial situation continued deteriorating. A November 18, 1958, financial report showed N.A.N.I. had borrowed $113,400 ($1 million in 2019 dollars) from the Druillard Trust between August 12, 1952, to November 15, 1954, of which $78,000 ($691,320.21 in 2019 dollars) was way past due. The trust was willing to grant a moratorium on the current notes but wanted $1,000 in monthly payments on $45,000 in older notes in a March 3, 1959, memorandum.

"It was stated by the N.A.N.I. officers that the institution is in no position to start a major payment program at this time due to the fact that for the next four months we are obligated to make $5,000/month payments to the Third National Bank," an April 30, 1959, memorandum stated.

On December 3, 1958, the American City Bureau of Chicago made four fundraising recommendations:

1. Separate business action of college from hospital.
2. Establish an advisory board of twelve to fifteen carefully selected business and professional men from the Nashville area.
3. Become part of the larger community such as the Chamber of Commerce and participate in the United Givers campaign.
4. Delay solicitation for a year, but initiate an effective public relations program, then consult them a year later about solicitation.

The year 1959 began with no fundraising program, the board deciding whether or not to hire a fundraising organization to do it, and unveiling a plan to raise $1 million within thirty-five to forty months for project one of a four-phase project. Drawing plans, fundraising, and building construction would begin immediately.

The board was still trying to answer basic questions, all of which distracted energy from raising money.

Are we willing to set up an advisory committee, made up on prominent citizens of the community, to serve during the period of fundraising and during the period of construction?
Are we going to employ a fundraising organization to conduct the campaign for securing funds?
Are we willing to accept Hillbutton (government) funds if they are available?
Are we willing to borrow any money, such as federal funds that might be available on a long-term basis at 4.6 percent interest?

The board voted to plan for a 250-bed hospital building on March 3, 1959, and targeted five possible sources of funding: N.A.N.I. Alumni Association, medical staff, Southern Union and Kentucky-Tennessee Conferences of SDA, and the community.

Money owed to the Druillard Trust complicated the program. N.A.N.I. had paid $41,000 on the loan prior to 1954 but could now pay only the interest on a $113,000 balance. A $5,000/month obligation to the Third National Bank drained their resources. Nevertheless, the board moved forward with a public announcement of a $3 million development program, phase one including two two-story buildings, each housing fifty patients. A third building would be a one-story physical therapy structure. Construction would start May 1, 1960.

"This new construction is long overdue," read the announcement in the March 1960 *Madison Survey*. "The original frame buildings that were constructed 50 years ago are still in use, but they are badly worn and need to be replaced. The Joint Commission on Accreditation of Hospitals has stated that Madison must begin new fire-proof construction as soon as possible and must make existing quarters more fire-safe."

This same issue showed a picture taken after a luncheon of the Madison Rotary Club and top hospital officers in front of an artist's sketch of the building. "Community leaders and groups from Madison and Nashville are showing great interest in the plans for the new hospital. Civic clubs and business organizations are meeting on the campus for luncheons."

The July 1960 survey announced that Robert W. Morris had become the new hospital administrator. At an October 17, 1960, constituency meeting, Treasurer James Blair reported bills payable amounted to $20,000 for the sanitarium and hospital and $103,000 from the college, with no provision for paying off this debt. Separating the hospital and college provided for current operating expenses but not enough to cover the back bills.

While the hospital publicly announced the construction of a new building, no actual work on it started during 1960.

Chapter 7

The Final Blow

The board of directors elected Ralph Davidson president of N.A.N.I. on February 10, 1961. Davidson, then serving as treasurer of Southern Missionary College (now Southern Adventist University), was a graduate of Madison College, had taught there, as well as Walla Walla College, and had been a partner in an accounting firm in Murfreesboro, Tennessee, doing some auditing for the institution in the past. He quickly learned that he had an emergency situation on his hands. On his first day in office, he received unexpected news. "I got a phone call from the State of Tennessee saying we will give you one year to build a new hospital building or we are going to close it down," he said in a September 2001 interview. "I didn't know what to do. If the hospital closed, it would wipe out the college."

And that was not all.

Hospital Administrator Robert W. Morris unveiled another first-magnitude crisis in an open letter to the Layman Foundation dated August 4, 1961. The "other hospital" in Madison was becoming a reality. "We are faced for the first time with a threat to our existence by the erection of a $3 million 150-bed institution that will be supported by this community and the Federal Government," he wrote.

The community physicians thus might or might not support Madison Hospital in the future. Morris then estimated that of the Adventist physicians—Elmer Bottsford, Roy Bowes, Fred Cothren, H.F. Evans, Julian C. Gant, Charles Gillett, G.W. Johnson, C.E. Kendall, J.W. Osborne, and Jean Slate—six of them would be gone by 1965 for various reasons.

He also pointed out the need for new college and hospital buildings—especially hospital—and suggested the development of campus industries to relieve the college of reliance on hospital subsidies. "The time for action is NOW," he emphasized. "I envision only a three-year period before the other institution makes inroads on our income."

The hospital took action immediately. Davidson negotiated a $2 million bond issue to build a new hospital building, knowing it would close the college. On July 5, 1961, board of directors approved a smaller-than-original plan but of sufficient size to maintain accreditation of the hospital and its several affiliated training courses. They were now paying the price for not initiating a proper fundraising campaign in the early 1950s. With community support now going over to the "other hospital," the only option was to borrow the money.

The March 4, 1962, constituency meeting viewed an artist's sketch of a new hospital building to be done in two phases—first phase $1.4 million and the second phase $1 million. By September 20, 1962, it was announced at a board of trustees meeting that the hospital had received $500,000 from Hill-Burton funds, assuring construction of a second 260-bed hospital wing with a modern, well-equipped physiotherapy section as well as kitchen and dining service.

The college, meanwhile, was sinking. Enrollment for the 1962-63 school year was down, meaning a $100,000 deficit. Madison Foods also reported a $107,000 debt. The board, at its September 20, 1962, meeting, saw four alternatives:

1—Close the college and have hospital schools only
2—Revert to the junior college level
3—Develop a technological school
4—Become an extension of Southern Missionary College

> *The original objective of supplying competent, self-sacrificing people to staff the self-supporting units had died out.*

The original objective of supplying competent, self-sacrificing people to staff the self-supporting units had died out.

The October 5, 1962, board of trustees meeting acknowledged that paying all the bills and at the same time developing accredited college programs had become an unsolvable problem, at least so far. The July 1962 financial statement showed a liability of $547,000 ($4.25 million in 2019) "and generally a very precarious financial situation."

By December 1962, the college picture looked grim indeed, with fourteen of sixteen departments showing a loss of more than $75,000 with slight possibility for improvement during the next year. Charles Fleming, business manager of Southern Missionary College, suggested that Madison might fill a denominational need for a technical school. But without a denominational wage scale, sustentation eligibility, top financial management, and recognition, it would be hard to obtain competent personnel.

The year 1963 began with a delegation consisting of D.R. Rees, K.F. Ambs, and K.C. Beem from the Southern Union office presenting Madison's problems and proposition to General Conference officers. The church leaders appreciated the profound contribution of Madison and its major role in the Southern Union going from being a largely underprivileged Adventist mission field in 1904 to becoming one of the strongest unions in the North American Division, both financially and in membership. The General Conference had made a $30,000 gift to the institution but hoped that the board and constituency could find another way to operate it successfully.

The Layman Foundation Board of Trustees suggested downsizing the education to eleventh and twelfth grades in addition to the nurses course, medical records, X-ray and laboratory. At the February 3, 1963, constituency meeting, Ralph M. Davidson resigned after serving two years as president.

The good news was that soy milk from Madison Foods showed a net profit of $1,578.99 though developing it had cost a lot.

The college, however, had lost $65,000 during the year or $5,000 per month. During the past year, the college received a final $32,000 subsidy from the hospital. In addition, the institution sold thirty acres of land for $32,000 which went into operating expenses, so the actual loss for the year was $115,000 instead of $65,000.

At the fifth annual meeting of the Association of Seventh-day Adventist Self-supporting Institutions, (A.S.I.) held at Campion Academy, Loveland, Colorado, August 13-16, 1952, Madison College President A.A. Jasperson told the group that institutions must surmount their problems as they come. "Unless they do this, the problems become insurmountable," he said. "Then drastic changes have to be made—which is unfortunate."

That very thing had occurred at Madison during his administration, with the fundraising challenge for upgrading buildings on campus going unmet. Now, ten years later, the "drastic change" would be the college losing its hospital subsidy—a disastrous misfortune.

Chairman of the Board Don Rees summed it all up. Separation of the hospital from the college left it without a means to continue its existence. The industries have only added to the financial difficulties. With the college losing $5,000 a month by the end of the spring quarter it will take approximately $200,000-$250,000 to pay current obligations and losses.

The board has recommended to the constituency that the conference take over the institution and operate it.

The Southern Union Conference had helped in the form of appropriations, assisting with Bible teacher salaries and membership on the board and constituency, but hoped some other solution could be found. In his farewell address to the N.A.N.I. Constituency, President Davidson summed up the circumstances leading to the college running out of money and putting too much stress on him.

"Two years ago we set out upon the road to build a new hospital unit," he said. "This was made necessary because we were given only a one-year provisional accreditation for the hospital and were told definitely that unless we had some actual operations in motion within the next year, we would lose our accreditation altogether."

His predecessors had punted the fundraising effort, and now he had just one option. "We had already tried to put into effect a campaign to raise funds in the community but found that the business leaders had lost faith in us due to the repeated attempts to get a building program going and nothing coming of it; hence we brought to our board and constituency the bond program as the alternative."

This approach worked, netting an initial $500,000 in cash during the first issue, enabling the architect to come up with the first phase for hospital construction. A Hillburton grant from the Federal Government also gave them another $500,000. But obtaining the bond funds came at a price.

"In order, however, to obtain the bond issue, it was necessary for us to place a mortgage on the entire institution with the exception of the food factory and certain other areas such as the lease-homes by faculty members, as security for the bonds," Davidson continued. "It was also necessary to mortgage the income of the hospital beyond its operating expenses for the same purpose. This in itself created a problem for the college as the hospital had been subsidizing the college over the past years anywhere from $80,000 a year on down to $30,000. We were well aware that this meant that the college would have real problems as to its ability to finance its program."

The college found some source of outside income but not enough. "In order to accomplish this we raised tuition and tried to adjust the other expenses of the students, that they might care for their full share," he said. "We also applied to the conference for aid, and we are thankful that they saw fit to give us this current year $30,000 toward the operation of the school.

But the lack of money had rendered impossible the task of Madison College keeping up with the other denominational colleges in upgrading their programs to meet the needs of post-World War II-era students. "We do think that the instruction we have given has been of a high caliber, but we haven't been able to modernize our buildings or laboratories, nor to recruit staff in certain areas which would help to raise the standards of the instruction as much as we would like to see," he said.

They had tried advertising across the North American Division, but the union papers turned down these promotional requests due to a commitment to the colleges serving their own territories. A frustrated recruiting effort had resulted in fewer students than the amount needed to balance the budget. Davidson anticipated a $75,000 shortfall for the school year ($628,850.49 in 2019).

The food factory had made some progress in soy milk research, but again the institution lacked the necessary funds to develop it properly. He recommended leasing it out to a private enterprise agreeing to employ student labor. The financial situation looked impossible. Liabilities had increased from $85,000 in 1960 to a present $110,000. The net worth had gone down $64,000 during that same time. "This has resulted from our inability to recruit students and keep our enrollment up to where we could manage the college without losses," Davidson said. "This includes the losses on the farm and other departments, which I feel are quite largely owing to the fact that we are trying to run them as educational programs rather than as industries. This would not be true of the food factory."

He concluded that the situation was so bad that it would take a stronger organization than the SDA denomination to make the college run successfully. Davidson finished by saying the superhuman stress of the situation had forced him into resignation. "I am sorry to have to announce that upon the advice of my personal physician, and also that of two other doctors whose counsel I regard very highly, I have resigned my position here as president of the N.A.N.I. and also as president of the college, as well as my membership on the Board of Trustees. I have given this considerable thought and feel that this must be done or it may be that I would soon be in a position where I would not be able to give any service anywhere."

The N.A.N.I. Constituency voted at that meeting to ask the Southern Union Conference to assume ownership and control of the Madison college, hospital, and food factory. The union executive committee accepted this request four days later, and the General Conference Committee gave full official approval on April 4.

Chapter 8

The End

On May 1, 1963, Horace R. Beckner, church and institutional secretary of the Georgia-Cumberland Conference of SDAs based in Atlanta, Georgia, accepted the presidency of Madison College. He had previously served as an academy principal and pastor-evangelist.

One of the first things he did was to ask for money, saying the General, union, and local conference had voted to give the school $50,000 for the coming year as seed for raising another $25,000 needed immediately for repairs.

"In order to carry forward the work of God here in this place, it will be necessary to make major repairs on practically all of the buildings," he wrote in introducing himself to *Madison Survey* readers. "New roofs, gutters, painting, and repairs of all kinds is needed in order to take care of the students that must be trained for the finishing of God's work, and housing for our workers. Any amount will be greatly appreciated, from a dollar to thousands."

The work cannot be finished by ministers alone. Above all, we need more consecrated laymen.

Perhaps he should have gone in as president during the early 1950s. In the June 1963 *Madison Survey*, Beckner wrote about the need of the denomination for a technical school. "We need a combination. The work will not be finished until we all work together. The work cannot be finished by ministers alone. Above all, we need more consecrated laymen."

Work started immediately on improving the College Press, cafeteria kitchen, and dormitories. "Madison is depending on you, the alumni, former students, teachers, and other friends of the college, to show your loyalty and devotion by having a part in the great improvement program that must be done in order for us to continue the work of God here in this place."

The 1963-64 school year started with work being done on the Helen Funk Assembly Hall, Williams Hall (girls' dormitory), and Kinsey apartments. Enrollment stood at 226 full-time students and another 20 part-time attendees. Groundbreaking for the new hospital building took place on October 31, and earthmovers began excavation on November 13. Then came the fatal body blow.

On November 6, 1963, the state of Tennessee withdrew accreditation of the nursing education program. The state allowed the senior students in the class of 1964 to sit for their state boards, but that would be all. The school of nursing was the keystone in the arch. Closing it threatened all the other programs, even the hospital.

In a February 6, 1964, meeting, after an all-day look at the financial situation of the school board it was voted "that following the spring quarter, all offerings of Madison College be suspended, and the school of nursing program be completely transferred to the hospital, and be continued and strengthened as a hospital school."

That action galvanized the alumni into organizing a full-fledged fundraising campaign. Bernard Bowen, president of the alumni association, and Lawrence Bidwell, president of the nursing chapter pleaded with the Southern Union Committee to find a way to come up with enough money to keep Madison going.

"At the meeting the board chairman, Elder Don Rees, told those present that the union committee had big ears; that they wanted to be open minded, and not do anything hastily," stated the *Madison Survey* report of the meeting. "He stated that there have been repeated warnings since 1953, and two years ago we came near losing everything at Madison."

The alumni agreed to ask their members to raise $300,000 ($2.4 million in 2019) during the next six years for capital improvements and debt reduction. The board decided at its March 12 meeting to continue operation of the school. But that would mean increasing conference subsidies from $75,000 to $115,000.

The alumni decided to invest their energy in raising money for a new girls' dormitory and to transform Williams Hall into a boys' dormitory. "The Alumni Association realizes that more positive financial support of the college should have been forthcoming from the alumni through its association all these years," Lawrence Bidwell wrote in the Survey. He suggested a "living endowment" as a means of supporting the school. He asked that the alumni give $200,000 to meet this need. He encouraged all alumni chapters to talk about this need and encourage their members to give.

"The Southern Union Conference and General Conference will contribute $116,000 in operating funds for the next year, but capital improvements is the responsibility of the alumni if our college is to continue," he wrote. But closing the nursing school turned out to be too much. Interest in the nursing program was high, but Madison received a minimal response to a vocational school proposal.

The board thus decided to close the college and merge the nursing program with that of Southern Missionary College (now Southern Adventist University). They would offer a two-year associate degree in nursing along with several paramedical courses. The hospital needed an accredited school of nursing and vice versa.

To raise money for an adequate facility, the board voted to sell 300 acres of farmland to erect a building including rooms for 180 students, three classrooms, seven instructors' offices, and a library. The campus was divided between the Kentucky-Tennessee Conference, which would operate a boarding academy, and the hospital, which would own all the new educational facilities being erected by the Southern Union. Worthington Foods took over the food factory, and the industries went to the academy, which started the 1964-65 school year in the Science Building, Demonstration Building, and Williams Hall.

During the 1964 turmoil, former President Arthur A. Jasperson spoke of the work established at Madison sixty years before as a "very simple work." "The only virtues we had were that we were very happy and very poor," he said. "This institution is going to write a new chapter."

Going from poverty to respectability had proved counterproductive.

The Kentucky-Tennessee Conference took over the academy, initially operating it as a boarding school, then closed the dormitories and transformed it into a day school serving the greater Nashville area churches.

The hospital continued its operations as part of the Kentucky-Tennessee Conference, which turned it over to the Adventist Health System in 1975 with Homer Grove as administrator. Others following him were Bob Trimble, Jim Boyle, Bill Haupt, Clint Krietner, Don Jernigan, and Jim Bunch.

The "other hospital" in Madison, developed as a result of the delay in fundraising on campus, opened as Nashville Memorial Hospital and turned out to be serious competition. The Hospital Corporation of America (HCA), based in Nashville, bought out the hospital and later moved it to a more prominent location along I-65 and renamed it Skyline Medical Center. This same organization announced the purchase of the hospital, now known as Tennessee Christian Medical Center, on December 21, 2004, with the sale finalized April 1, 2005.

Epilogue

And so the original Madison died. As the generation of Old Testament Israelites following Joshua failed to subdue the remaining Canaanites, so the new Madison generation found itself unable, for one reason or another, to maintain the unique Nashville Agricultural and Normal Institute, and it evolved into a hospital and school with little difference from other institutions of its type.

The farm shut down. The college became a conference academy, initially housing boarding students and then a day school serving the Nashville area Adventist churches. Madison Hospital changed its name to Tennessee Christian Medical Center and operated for another forty years as a regular community hospital, eventually becoming part of the giant Hospital Corporation of America. Madison Foods united with Worthington Foods.

Yet the heritage lives on, and missionary-minded school, agricultural, and medical enterprises still operate—mostly on a smaller scale than Madison. Adventists doing self-supporting work look to the Madison model for guidance and inspiration. Visitors come wanting to see the campus based on what they have heard about Madison.

This raises the question: Could the generation following E.A. Sutherland have saved Madison?

I think so.

Worthy enterprises, like old Madison with a mission in the South, have a history of attracting donors. Rich women like Josephine Gotzain and Lida Funk Scott invested a substantial part of their personal fortunes in the work of Madison during its early years. In 1940, according to the December 10, 1941, *Madison Survey*, the campus needed a new dormitory. Mr. Edgar Williams and his wife of Bradford, PA, guests of the Madison Sanitarium for several weeks, gave a large donation for a girls' dormitory under construction because of their interest in self-supporting work. A $15,000 gift (the equivalent of about $264,092.86 in 2019) from the Nashville business community had enabled the work to begin, aided by another $8,000 ($140,849.52 in 2019) from the General Conference of Seventh-day Adventists. Designers allotted space for a new college cafeteria. "In an almost miraculous manner," the school obtained the necessary equipment for completion, thanks in part to the students responding to a challenge to raise $1,000 ($17,606.19 in 2021 dollars). Local and union Adventist conferences gave generously, and Dr. Floyd Bralliar solicited much of the rest from various individuals. Estimated value of the building stood at $40,000 (or $704,247.62 now).

This kind of fundraising did not continue through the late forties and early fifties, even though the April 30, 1947, *Madison Survey* announced an estimated $560,000 need ($6.5 million in 2021) and the board of directors appointed a committee to start organizing a campaign to raise the money.

A photograph in the fiftieth anniversary album, published in 1954 to celebrate a half century of successful ministry, pictured a fundraising committee organized to raise $75,000 (the equivalent of $726,997.19 now) for married students' housing. Several prominent Nashvillians are part of the group. Jack C. Massey, who started out as a pharmacist, developed a chain of six drug stores in Nashville and went on to co-found the Hospital Corporation of America (HCA). R.D. Herbert, Jr., owned a roofing company. Norris Maffett was prominent in the insurance business. Andrew Bell Benedict was a top officer at First American National Bank. William Sandborn, W.E. Patterson, and Felix A. Lorenz represented Madison.

This commemorative yearbook, displaying the impact Madison had made through its people, did not reflect the desperate financial situation of the home base struggling under a $65,000 debt (or $625,379.74 in 2021).

Did Dr. Sandborn and Mr. Patterson ask these businesspeople for help in clearing this big debt? Did they tell them that helping the hospital with some of its needs would enable it to maintain accreditation and thus keep up its college subsidy? Both institutions served important economic needs of the community.

My contention is that if they would put money into married students' housing, they would have also contributed to the rescue of a hospital and college.

At least some prominent Nashvillians went on record praising Madison.

"Since its founding nearly 50 years ago, Madison College and Sanitarium-Hospital has seldom asked for help," commented E.B. Stahlman, president of the Nashville Chamber of Commerce and a top officer of the Nashville *Banner*. "This community, of which this institution is an important and integral part, has sometimes overlooked this most worthy and inspiring enterprise that is known far and wide as the only truly self-supporting college in the United States."

"You have become an important member of our college group that has brought to Nashville the title 'The Athens of the South,'" commented Parkes Armistad, president of First American National Bank. "We wish for your continued success in your undertakings and the contributions you are making to the life of this Community."

The Honorable Gov. Frank G. Clement commented, "It is refreshing to find a college operating on a self-supporting basis. The State of Tennessee needs more schools like Madison College."

And then Madison College had its share of successful, high-income alumni. E.A. Sutherland's large investment through his biggest donor in the struggling young College of Medical Evangelists during the year back in 1915-25 had paid off handsomely. Some of his students had come back to Madison and Middle Tennessee as doctors and were succeeding big time.

My father, Dr. Albert G. Dittes, was one of them, building up a flourishing medical practice in nearby Portland, Tennessee. He owed a lot to Madison and wanted to help there. But nobody from there ever came and asked him for money.

Several other Madison alumni like him were successful medical professionals along with some non-Madison physicians in the area.

The burdens borne by the Advent pioneers like James and Ellen White were just as heavy for the generation following them, like E.A. Sutherland and Percy T. Magan, and they have not lessened.

"We are receiving a blessing from this work, and pray that more schools may be established in needy places of the South," young Professor Sutherland had written in 1910. "Many young men and women should seek such an experience as these young people are having. Our failure to go in and possess the land is a disregard of the principles that the Lord has given us."

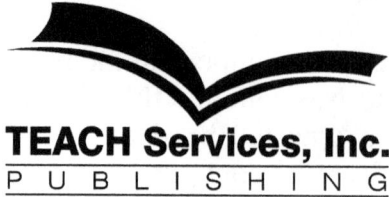

www.ingramcontent.com/pod-product-compliance
Lightning Source LLC
Chambersburg PA
CBHW071751090426
42738CB00011B/2636